Project Editor: Ronna Simpson

The illustrations in this book were rendered in watercolor.

Library of Congress Catalog Card Number: 98-91601

ISBN 0-9664050-0-5

Prospect Hill Company
61 Prospect Street
Brockton, MA 02301

Printed in Korea

The Gift of a Snowflake

TIMOTHY McMULLEN

Illustrated by William Beyer

Prospect Hill Company, Brockton, Massachusetts

Dedication

For my son, Ryan,
my forever friend,
know you can always count on me.

For my daughter, Kaylen,
my lucky star,
you have won my heart with your
sweet and wonderful ways.

Both of you have made my life complete.

One day, long, long ago, a young angel named Kaylen asked God why He had made all the angels the same.

God replied, "My dear Kaylen, all angels are different. They may look alike but they are different in many ways.

Some are quiet,

some like to play games,

some like to read,

and some just like to rest.

Everyone in heaven and on earth is unique because of the individual, special qualities that I give them.

Everyone is created for a purpose."

Kaylen questioned God again, asking: "Am I different from the other angels?"

"You, Kaylen, are different in many ways. First of all," God answered, laughing, "you ask more questions than any of the other angels, but that is good!"

"What is *my* purpose?" the young angel wanted to know. "That question will be answered when I give you a gift," God said.
"A gift!!" Kaylen exclaimed.

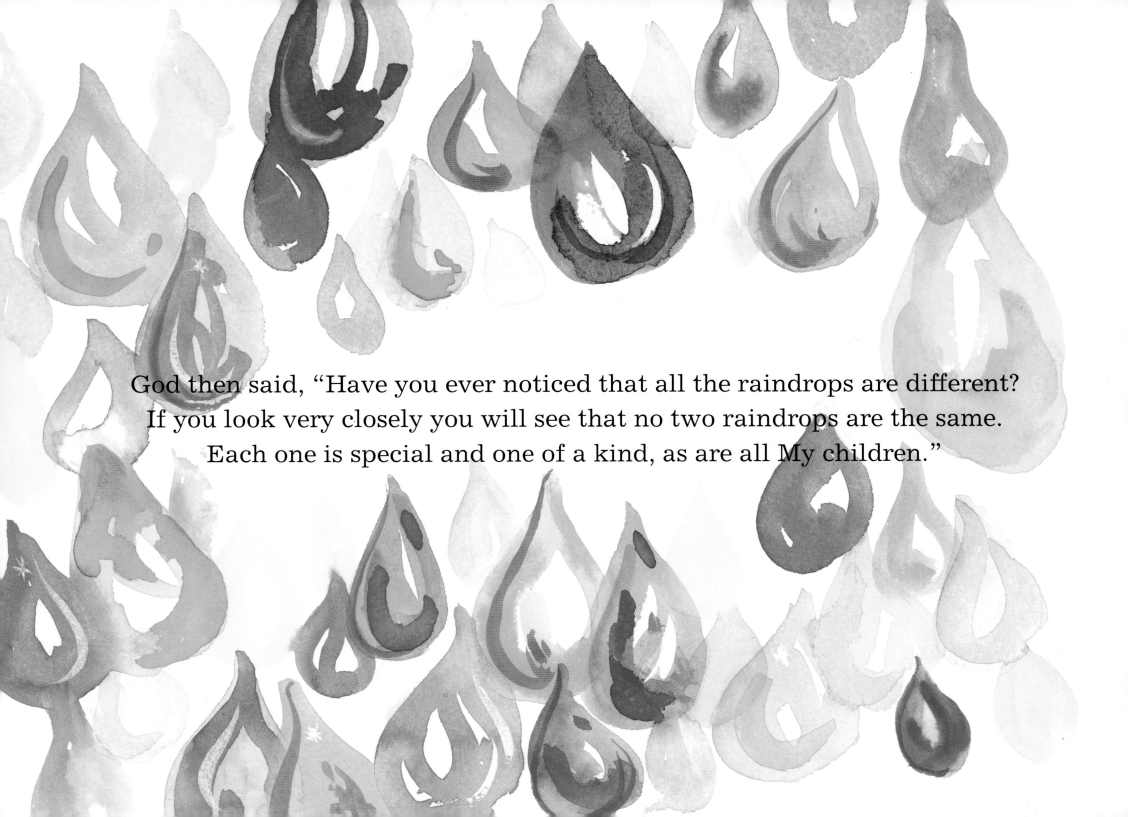

God then said, "Have you ever noticed that all the raindrops are different? If you look very closely you will see that no two raindrops are the same. Each one is special and one of a kind, as are all My children."

The doubting angel replied, "I know You love the raindrops, God, but to me, they all look the same."

"On Christmas morning," God continued, "I will give you a special gift and then you will believe."

And so it came to pass.

On Christmas morning, the day God's only Son, Jesus, was born,
the rain appeared.

God commanded, "Let it be cold this day, so the rain will freeze and turn white like the clouds above."

The rain changed to frozen white shapes
and Kaylen was amazed!

and she even caught them on her tongue.

Remembering what God had told her she looked very closely and saw that God was right, no two shapes were exactly the same. Each shape was indeed different and unique.

The little young angel cried out with joy. "Blessed are You, Great God, for every drop of rain is different, just as You said!"

God smiled and asked, "Kaylen,
what shall we call this gift of yours, this frozen rain?"

What a beautiful gift!

She played with these frozen shapes

and she even caught them on her tongue.

Remembering what God had told her she looked very closely and saw
that God was right, no two shapes were exactly the same.
Each shape was indeed different and unique.

The little young angel cried out with joy. "Blessed are You, Great God, for every drop of rain is different, just as You said!"

God smiled and asked, "Kaylen,
what shall we call this gift of yours, this frozen rain?"

The angel realized now that one of her purposes was to name this new creation, her gift from God.

She thought long and hard

STARSBRIGHT

SKYMAGIC

PRETTIES

FLUFFS

FALLING STARS

COLORCHIPS

BRIGHT

REFLECTORS

DEEPFREEZERS

LOVELY FLAKES

Sparklers

HEAVEN DROPS

TWINKLEGLOWERS

and finally shouted, "Flakes, flakes of snow!"
We will call this gift
from God,

Snowflakes!

From that time on, God lets

the snowflakes fall each winter

to remind us that we are all Children of God, that we are unique in our own way and that each of us has been created...

... for a special purpose.